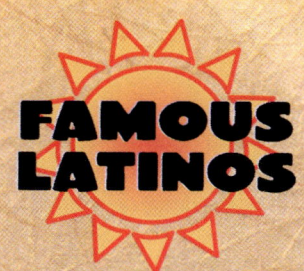

FAMOUS LATINOS

Roberto Clemente

Baseball Hero

Lila and Rick Guzmán

South Huntington Pub. Lib.
145 Pidgeon Hill Rd.
Huntington Sta., N.Y. 11746

Enslow Elementary
an imprint of
Enslow Publishers, Inc.

40 Industrial Road
Box 398
Berkeley Heights, NJ 07922
USA

http://www.enslow.com

Series Adviser
Bárbara C. Cruz, Ed.D., Series Consultant
Professor, Social Science Education
University of South Florida

Series Literacy Consultant
Allan A. De Fina, Ph.D.
Past President of the New Jersey Reading Association
Professor, Department of Literacy Education
New Jersey City University

Note to Parents and Teachers: The *Famous Latinos* series supports National Council for the Social Studies (NCSS) curriculum standards. The Words to Know section introduces subject-specific vocabulary words.

This series was designed by Irasema Rivera, an award-winning Latina graphic designer.

Enslow Elementary, an imprint of Enslow Publishers, Inc.

Enslow Elementary® is a registered trademark of Enslow Publishers, Inc.

Copyright © 2006 by Enslow Publishers, Inc.

All rights reserved.

No part of this book may be reproduced by any means without the written permission of the publisher.

Library of Congress Cataloging-in-Publication Data

Guzmán, Lila, 1952–
    Roberto Clemente : baseball hero / Lila and Rick Guzmán.
      p. cm. — (Famous Latinos)
    Includes index.
    ISBN 0-7660-2640-X
    1. Clemente, Roberto, 1934–1972. 2. Baseball players—Puerto Rico—Biography. I. Guzmán, Rick. II. Title. III. Series.
    GV865.C45G89 2006
    796.357092—dc22
                                        2005031731

Printed in the United States of America

10 9 8 7 6 5 4 3 2 1

To Our Readers
We have done our best to make sure all Internet addresses in this book were active and appropriate when we went to press. However, the author and the publisher have no control over and assume no liability for the material available on those Internet sites or on other Web sites they may link to. Any comments or suggestions can be sent by e-mail to comments@enslow.com or to the address on the back cover.

Every effort has been made to locate all copyright holders of material used in this book. If any errors or omissions have occurred, corrections will be made in future editions of this book.

Illustration Credits: © 2005 Jupiter Images Corporation, p. 9; AP/Wide World, pp. 11, 12, 14, 16, 17, 19, 20, 22R, 23, 26, 27, 28; Carnegie Library of Pittsburgh, p. 22L; Geoatlas @ 2000 Graphi-Ogre, p. 6; Library of Congress, p. 7; MLB Photos via Getty Images, pp. 4, 18, 24; National Baseball Hall of Fame Library, Cooperstown, NY, p. 8; US Postal Service, p. 13.

Cover Illustrations: AP/Wide World

Contents

1 Life in Puerto Rico 5

2 *¡Arriba!* Let's Go!. 10

3 Roberto Helps the Pirates 15

4 The 1971 World Series 21

5 Earthquake 25

   Timeline 29

   Words to Know 30

   Learn More About Roberto Clemente
   (Books and Internet Addresses). . . . 31

   Index 32

Roberto Clemente

❋ 1 ❋
Life in Puerto Rico

One day, a boy was walking past a ballpark. Suddenly, a baseball flew over the walls and landed at his feet. The boy picked it up and took it home. From then on, he slept with the baseball under his pillow. That boy was Roberto Clemente. He would grow up to become a famous baseball player—and the first Latino in the Baseball Hall of Fame. "I was born to play baseball," he once said.

Roberto Clemente was born on August 18, 1934, in Carolina, Puerto Rico. His father was Melchor Clemente, and his mother was Luisa Walker.

Roberto was born on the island of Puerto Rico.

Roberto was the youngest of eight children. His father worked on a sugar cane farm. Sugar is made from the sugar cane plant. His mother was busy taking care of the children. She also earned extra money for the family by sewing, cooking, and selling some groceries. In the Clemente home, everyone spoke Spanish. In Puerto Rico, Spanish is the main language.

Roberto was shy and respectful at school. His mother hoped he would go to college. As for Roberto, he dreamed only of playing baseball. He used tree branches or broomsticks for bats. He spent hours hitting soup cans and rocks. As a boy, Roberto did not have money to buy real bats and balls.

When Roberto was fourteen years old, he started playing on a baseball team for the Sello Rojo (SAY-yo ROH-hoh) rice company. Three years later, the Santurce (sahn-TOOR-say) Crabbers asked Roberto to play for them. The Crabbers were the best team in Puerto Rico.

Roberto and his family lived in a shack like this one.

Roberto in his Crabbers (Cangrejeros) uniform.

In 1954, a man came to Puerto Rico looking for new baseball players. He was a scout for the Brooklyn Dodgers, a team in New York City. He watched Roberto play. *Thwack!* Roberto hit the ball over the fence. *Zoom!* He raced around the bases. *Whoosh!* Roberto's powerful arm shot the ball across the field.

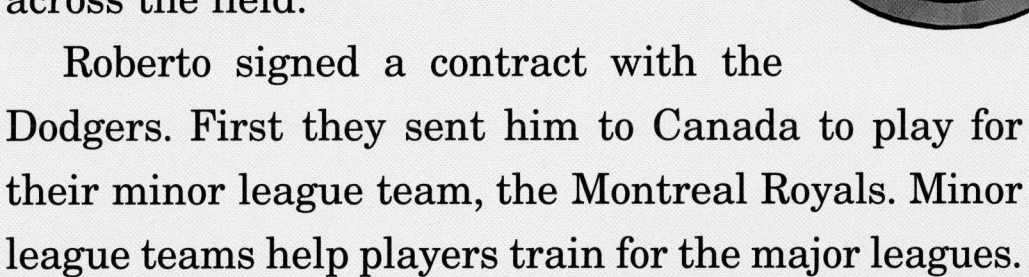

Roberto signed a contract with the Dodgers. First they sent him to Canada to play for their minor league team, the Montreal Royals. Minor league teams help players train for the major leagues.

When a baseball scout for the Pittsburgh Pirates went to Canada, he saw Roberto practice. The baseball draft was coming up. That is when teams pick their new players. The Pittsburgh Pirates were the worst team in the National League. They were in last place, so they were given first choice in the baseball draft.

They chose Roberto.

✷ 2 ✷

¡Arriba! Let's Go!

Roberto played his first game for the Pittsburgh Pirates on April 17, 1955. When he was not on the ballfield, Roberto often felt lonely in Pittsburgh. He missed Puerto Rican food, such as fried plantains (a kind of banana), rice, beans, and steak. He was homesick for Puerto Rico's warm weather. Roberto missed the Spanish language, too. He did not speak English very well.

Like many Puerto Ricans, Roberto had dark skin. He soon discovered that dark-skinned people were treated badly in the United States in the 1950s.

Roberto joined the Pittsburgh Pirates.

Roberto was shocked to find signs that kept people apart by the color of their skin.

In those days, there were separate restaurants and hotels for blacks and whites. This was a problem when the Pirates were on the road, traveling to other ballparks. Many places, especially in the South, did not serve blacks. Roberto and others had to wait on the team bus while the white players went inside to eat and sleep.

Roberto was angry. He said it was wrong to treat people differently because of their skin color. "I don't believe in color; I believe in people," he said. At that time, it was unusual for a star athlete to speak out the way Roberto did. Some people did not like it.

Newspaper reporters made fun of Roberto because he did not speak English very well. They also wrote that he complained too much. They called him lazy on the days when he said he was hurt and could not play baseball.

Yet Roberto's troubles were real. Sometimes he was in terrible pain. He had hurt his back in a car accident. Playing baseball, he also hurt his elbow and neck.

From 1955 to 1960, Roberto worked hard to become a better player. He was very popular with the fans. Sometimes he signed autographs for three hours after a game. His fans saw that he loved baseball and always tried his best. When it was his turn to bat, they yelled: *"¡Arriba!"* Let's go!

With Roberto's help, the Pirates became a better team. By 1960, they were on their way to the World Series for the first time in thirty-five years. The future looked bright for Roberto and the Pirates.

Roberto always enjoyed talking to his fans.

3

Roberto Helps the Pirates

For the 1960 World Series, the Pirates were facing the New York Yankees. The Pirates had not won the World Series since 1925. The Yankees had won it eight times. Everyone thought the Yankees would win.

A team must win four games to win the series. After six games, the Yankees and Pirates had three wins each. That made the next game very exciting. In the ninth inning, the score was 9–9. At the last minute, with a fantastic home run, the Pirates won the game. They were the World Series champions!

The fans went wild and ran onto the field. Roberto was very happy. He had played very well in all seven games. He batted in three runs and did not make any mistakes out in the field.

Each winter at the end of the regular baseball season, Roberto went home to Puerto Rico. There, he played baseball in the Winter League. One day, Roberto was shopping in a drugstore in Carolina, Puerto Rico. He saw a young woman named Vera Cristina Zabala. The two started dating, and a year later, on November 14, 1964, they married. Over the years, they had three sons, Roberto Jr., Luis, and Enrique.

Roberto and Vera on their wedding day.

For Roberto, the most important things in life were family, children, and baseball. He made a lot of money playing baseball and was very generous with it. He bought a new home for his parents. He gave money to poor children and often visited children in hospitals. In Puerto Rico, he taught many youngsters how to play baseball.

People loved to watch Roberto play baseball. He was good at everything. He could hit, run, field and throw. As a right fielder, he made many amazing catches.

A family portrait: Roberto with his parents, wife, and sons.

Sometimes he dived into the grass. Other times, he made a spectacular jump into the air. Once, he saw a ball coming toward him. He turned and ran to catch it. *Smack!* He hit a concrete wall. There was silence in the park. Then Roberto raised his left arm. He had caught the ball. The crowd cheered. An ambulance took him to the hospital, where he got stitches in his chin.

Roberto was famous for the way he threw a ball. He made it shoot across the field. Because he was a great fielder, he was named a Gold Glove outfielder every year he played. The Gold Glove is an award that honors the best fielders in the

Roberto's powerful arm sent the baseball flying across the field.

National League and the American League. From 1961 to 1972, Roberto won the Gold Glove twelve times. Roberto was also a good batter. Then, after he hit the ball, he ran to first base with lightning speed.

Roberto won many other awards and honors, too. In 1966, he was named the Most Valuable Player. He was the first Puerto Rican to win that award. To Roberto, it was the best honor a baseball player could receive. The same year, he was named National League Player of the Year.

In 1971, the Pirates made it to the World Series again. Roberto was ready for the excitement.

Roberto was a great right fielder. "I try to catch everything in the ballpark," he said.

Roberto once said that he wanted "to be remembered as a ballplayer who gave all he had to give."

4

The 1971 World Series

In the 1971 World Series, the Pittsburgh Pirates were playing the Baltimore Orioles. Everyone thought the Orioles would win. More than 60 million people watched the games on television. Roberto was playing his best. He hit .414. This was amazing because the Orioles pitchers were terrific, and many batters could not get a hit. Roberto was at bat twenty-nine times and had twelve hits. All of them were safe. He had two home runs and four RBIs. He made an important throw in game six that kept a runner on

"This World Series is the greatest thing that ever happened to me in baseball," said Roberto in 1971.

third base from scoring. Roberto was the star of the World Series. He was named the Most Valuable Player.

By the end of the World Series, it was clear that Roberto was one of the best baseball players of all time. People called him "El Grande," the Great One.

Roberto had one more goal. He wanted to hit 3,000. By September 30, 1972, Roberto had 2,999 hits. He needed only one more. He picked up the bat and looked at the pitcher. Everyone in the stadium waited. Would Roberto make the hit? Yes! The fans went crazy. Until then, only ten men in the history of

Roberto makes his 3,000th hit.

Roberto's 17 Years in the Majors	
Hits	3,000
RBIs	1,305
Average	.317
Games Played	2,433
Runs Scored	1,416
Doubles	440
Triples	166
Home Runs	240

baseball had hit the ball 3,000 times. Now Roberto was the eleventh.

Roberto had been playing major league baseball for seventeen years—from 1955 to 1972. He played for only one team: the Pittsburgh Pirates. By the end of the 1972 baseball season, Roberto had an amazing record.

✺ 5 ✺

Earthquake

On December 23, 1972, an earthquake shook the country of Nicaragua in Central America. The capital city was destroyed. Thousands of people died. Thousands of people lost their homes.

Roberto was home in Puerto Rico when he heard the news. He wanted to help. He went door-to-door asking for money and food for the earthquake victims. By the end of the week, he had enough supplies to fill an airplane. He had collected $150,000 and twenty-six tons of food, clothing, and medicine.

On New Year's Eve, December 31, 1972, Roberto was ready to fly to Nicaragua. The plane took off, carrying Roberto and four others, along with all the

Roberto wanted to help the people in Nicaragua.

supplies they had collected. Suddenly, an engine stopped working. There was a fire in the engine.

The pilot decided to go back to the airport. But it was too late. There was a loud explosion. As the plane turned left, it fell into the ocean. It was only half a mile away from Puerto Rico. Everyone on the plane died.

Deep-sea divers searched underwater for the people who had been on the plane. Roberto was never found. His tragic death stunned fans all over the world.

Puerto Ricans were very sad. They tied black ribbons to their front doors.

Roberto Clemente was only thirty-eight years old when he died. His three sons were seven, five, and four.

Usually, a baseball player has to wait five years after his last game to be voted into the Baseball Hall of Fame. Baseball officials changed the rules—just for Roberto. He became part of the Hall of Fame on March 20, 1973.

This statue at Pittsburgh's Three Rivers Stadium honors Roberto.

Roberto's son Luis, left, widow Vera, and son Roberto Jr. present a giant cereal box that honors Roberto. On Roberto Clemente Day, every year in September, baseball clubs collect money to help people in need, and the Roberto Clemente Award is given to a ballplayer who works to help others.

Many Latino baseball fans still say, *"Me hace falta Roberto Clemente."* Many English-speaking fans agree: "I miss Roberto Clemente."

Today, everyone remembers Roberto Clemente as a great athlete who cared about others. Many people believe he was the best right fielder ever to play baseball. He is also famous for his big heart, because he was always reaching out to help other people.

Timeline

1934 Born on August 18 in Carolina, Puerto Rico.

1954 A baseball scout asks Roberto to play for the Brooklyn Dodgers.

1955 The Pittsburgh Pirates pick Roberto in the baseball draft.

1960 The Pirates win the World Series for the first time in thirty-five years.

1961 Roberto wins the first of twelve Gold Glove awards.

1964 Marries Vera Zabala on November 14.

1966 Voted Most Valuable Player of the Year.

1972 Makes his 3,000th hit.

1972 Dies on December 31 in a plane crash near San Juan, Puerto Rico.

1973 Is the first Latino voted into the Baseball Hall of Fame.

Words to Know

arriba—The Spanish word that is used for "Let's go!"

baseball draft—The way teams pick new players.

Baseball Hall of Fame—A museum for the history of baseball. It is in Cooperstown, New York.

baseball scouts—People looking to find new baseball players for a team.

minor league team—A team that prepares new players for the major leagues.

Most Valuable Player Award—An award that honors the player who contributed most to the team's success. It is given by the Baseball Writers Association of America.

National League and American League—The two professional baseball leagues in the United States.

RBI—Run batted in. After a batter hits the ball, he gets an RBI for each runner who scores.

Learn More

Books

Mara, Wil. *Roberto Clemente*. New York: Children's Press, 2005.

Marquez, Heron. *Roberto Clemente: Baseball's Humanitarian Hero*. Minneapolis, Minn.: Carolrhoda Books, 2004.

Winter, Jonathan. *Roberto Clemente: Pride of the Pittsburgh Pirates*. New York: Atheneum, 2005.

Internet Addresses

Roberto Clemente's official Web site
<http://www.robertoclemente21.com>

The official site of the Pittsburgh Pirates
<http://www.pirateball.com>

Index

A
American League, 19, 30

B
Baltimore Orioles, 21
baseball draft, 9, 30
Baseball Hall of Fame, 5, 27, 30
Brooklyn Dodgers, 9

C
Clemente, Enrique (son), 16, 27
Clemente, Luis (son), 16, 27, 28
Clemente, Melchor (father), 5, 6
Clemente, Roberto,
    awards and honors, 18–19, 22, 27, 28
    baseball statistics, 23–24
    childhood, 5–7
    early baseball, 5, 7, 9
    education, 6
    generosity, 16–17, 25, 28
    marriage, 16
    minor league baseball, 9
    plane crash, 25–26
Clemente, Roberto Jr. (son), 16, 27, 28
Crabbers (Cangrejeros), 7, 8

D
discrimination, 10, 12–13

G
Gold Glove, 18, 19

M
Montreal Royals, 9
Most Valuable Player (MVP), 19, 22, 30

N
National League, 9, 19, 30
National League Player of the Year, 19
New York Yankees, 15
Nicaragua earthquake, 25, 26

P
Pittsburgh Pirates, 9, 10, 11–15, 18, 19–24
Puerto Rico, 5–7, 9, 10, 16–17, 19, 25–27

S
Sello Rojo rice company, 7
sugar cane, 6

W
Walker, Louisa (mother), 5, 6
Winter League, 16
World Series,
    in 1960: 13, 15
    in 1971: 19, 21–22

Z
Zabala, Vera Christina (wife), 16, 28

JUL - 2 2010
2260